GARDENS

OF
VERSAILLES

by **Simone Hoog**
General Curator of the Estate

art
lys   :

Editorial co-ordination: Denis Kilian (Director, Éditions Art Lys)
Graphic design and layout: Martine Mène
Editorial follow-up and picture research: Christian Ryo
Production: Pierre Kegels

ISBN 2-85495-129-5

Date of printing: March 26, 2003
Legal deposit: April 2003
Printed by SPPI

CONTENTS

The gardens of Versailles, which once aroused the enthusiasm of Louis XIV's contemporaries, still continue to amaze visitors today by their scale, the vast perspectives combined with the different groves, the numerous sculptures, the variety of materials, the profusion of water, and the rich plant collection.

The first garden laid out by Jacques de Menours, between 1631 and 1636, around the hunting lodge built for Louis XIII by Philibert Le Roy, was considerably enlarged by Louis XIV after 1663. From that time on, the King became fascinated with Versailles, even though he only established his court there in 1682. His passion for Versailles would continue to grow until his death in 1715. When he was at Versailles, the King would walk in his garden every day, admiring, criticising and ordering changes. The royal books kept faithful accounts of the constant developments to the site and the large sums of money allocated to the gardens. The King took such an interest in and derived such pleasure from his gardens that, in 1689, he wrote *The Manner of Presenting the Gardens of Versailles*, the text of which had been revised, expanded and corrected five times by 1705.

Louis XIV adopted the comments that Félibien had made back in 1687: "One can see the gardens and all that is enclosed within the little park. However, since there is an infinite number of objects that catch the eye from all quarters, and since one is often at a loss as to which way one ought to go, it would be wise to follow the route that

Manuscript of
The Manner of Presenting
the Gardens of Versailles
written by Louis XIV.

I will mark out in order to see each part in succession more conveniently and without becoming weary."

Visitors today are faced with the same problem, which is now even more difficult since they lack many of the clues to understanding that which was more obvious for gentlemen of the 17th century, with regard to the architecture of the gardens, symbolism, the botanical varieties and the new techniques employed by the great innovators, Le Nôtre, François Francine, Abbé Picard, La Quintynie, the Perrault brothers, and Philippe de la Hire to name but a few.

While the château was increasing in size and the little park was being developed, Louis XIV used his gardens for several festivities, the main organisers of which being Henri de Gissey and Vigarani. The talents of Lully and Quinault, Molière and Racine would be on display under the watchful eye of Colbert. Accounts from these festivities, which often lasted several days, give an accurate description of the performances, balls, dinners, firework displays, and the sumptuous, temporary décor: in May 1662, for *Les Plaisirs de l'Ile Enchantée*; in July 1668, for the royal *Grand Divertissement*, and finally in July and August 1674, for the last of the great festivities.

Le Nôtre set about working on Versailles in 1663. He rigorously applied the laws of perspective and the optical principles with which he had become familiar to the formidable terrain. This explains the importance of the "parterres" and the "mirrors of water", along with the large canals extending the wide rectilinear avenues. The surrounding areas were left clear in order to emphasise the château. The terrace adorned with two water "parterres" is the starting point of the strongly emphasised, central axis of the garden, around which the secondary east-west

and north-south axes are arranged, intersecting the
wooded areas in which the groves may be found: these
served as a location for light meals, concerts or dances.
The variety and scale of the water effects, for which
Le Nôtre called on the Italian hydraulic engineers, the
Francine brothers, completely changed the appearance
of the groves and strove to elicit the surprise and admira-
tion of spectators.

In the same way that he explored all the different possi-
bilities of water, Le Nôtre experimented with the contrasts
between light and dark, as visitors go from shady paths
into areas full of light. The trellis-work and tall, pruned
hedgerows forming walls of greenery, against which stand
white marble statues, and the rigorous symmetry of the
groups around the central axis, are balanced by the fantas-
tical nature of the groves and the yew trees trimmed in the
most striking styles of the topiary art, planted around the
parterres. The very scale of the terrain led Le Nôtre to
reshape the land entrusted to him: while he used the
natural slope of the site in the northern part of the
Versailles park, along the main east-west axis he transformed it by creating the great stairway leading to the
Fountain of Latona below, and in the south by the two
levels of the South Parterre and the Orangery. Le Nôtre's
art is a skilful balance between the symmetry of the different groups and axes, and fantasy in the details.

Le Nôtre used water to such a skilful effect that his
work in certain groves, such as the *Trois Fontaines*, may be
described as aquatic architecture; however, water was a

*Model of a trimmed shrub
in the Royal Avenue,
early 18th century.*

*View of the pump
and aqueduct at Marly,
by P.-D. Martin, 1724.*

*Perspective of the north-south axis
from the Fountain of Neptune,
by J.-B. Martin, 1696.*

*View of the gardens
and the château from the Fountain
of Apollo at the start of the reign
of Louis XVI.*

constant concern at Versailles due to the need to drain and dry out the unproductive and often marshy land, and the desire to supply the numerous fountains adorning the park. The digging of the Grand Canal, the Royal Island (now the King's Garden) and the Pond of the Swiss between 1668 and 1688, represented part of the drainage project.

Installation of the fountains resulted in larger and larger reservoirs being built. After the great pump erected by fountain-maker Denis Jolly in 1664, to draw water from the Clagny ponds, three reservoirs were built in 1667, on the site of the future northern wing of the château, which would remain until 1684.

The pump at Marly, which would carry water from the Seine via the Louveciennes aqueduct, was built between 1681 and 1684. However, this extraordinary machine, designed by Arnold de Ville and Rennequin Sualem, was unable to supply enough water. Thus, from 1684, water from the Eure was to be diverted to Versailles via a series of canals and aqueducts (remains of which may still be found in Maintenon and Buc), an immense project, mobilising thousands of men, which was suspended during the war with the League of Augsburg in 1689.

"An extraordinary network consisting of strings of ponds representing a surface area of 817 hectares and 168 km of channels was constructed to drain 8.5 million cubic metres of water over an area of 15,000 hectares." (Philippe Lardellier, 1993).

Today, the large reservoirs from Montbauron, the North (along Rue des Réservoirs), the Picardy coast, and Le Trèfle to Trianon still remain, supplemented by the Pond of the Swiss, which collects spring water from the Satory plateau, and the Grand Canal in particular.

"The sparkling fountains in the groves of Versailles use such vast quantities of water when they all play at the same time that, in the summer, only the water parterres and a few of the fountains visible from the château and terraces will normally play from ten o'clock in the morning to eight o'clock in the evening, while the King is in residence, so that the *Grandes-Eaux* will only play on the day of Pentecost and the feast day of St. Louis, or when an ambassador or highly respected representative from abroad comes to visit the royal residence. The display lasts two and a half hours and uses 35,292 hogsheads (approximately 9460 cubic metres) of water," (Jean-François Blondel, Architecture Française, 1756).

Nowadays, the *Grandes-Eaux* use 5000 to 8000 cubic metres, and the *Petites Eaux*, 5000 to 6000 cubic metres.

The gardens of Versailles are an immense open-air sculpture museum dedicated to the 17th and 18th centuries. More than three hundred sculptures adorn the avenues, groves and crossroads, emphasising the vistas, and embellishing the fountains. The earliest works were cast in lead and were usually gilded or painted realistically. From

1674, marble statues from the Great Commission and also marble replicas of classical statues, sent by pupils from the French Academy in Rome, started to appear in front of the hedgerows. Finally, ten years later, the Keller brothers' magnificent bronzes came to adorn the fountains on the central terrace.

The subjects represented were mainly taken from Greek and Roman mythology; however, "there could be endless discussions to discover the origin of the iconographic programme of Versailles, and the texts; the memoirs of the time and the archives of the "*Petite Académie*" (predecessor of the *Académie des Inscriptions et des Belles-Lettres*) have kept their secret," (F. Souchal). Interpretation of all of the sculptures is practically impossible for visitors today, who are too unfamiliar with classical culture.

Apollo rising out of the waves to begin his daily course.

Nevertheless, the myth of Apollo, the sun god, was extensively illustrated and developed at Versailles. Louis XIV adopted the sun emblem and explained in his own words, "without paying too much attention to specific details of lesser importance, the motto that I have since kept, and that you see in so many places, should, in some way, represent the duties of a prince and eternally incite me to fulfil them. The sun is the chosen body which, according to the rules of the art, is the most noble of all, and which, through its uniqueness, through the brilliance that surrounds it, through the light that it conveys to the other stars which make up a court of sorts, through the equal and just distribution of light to all the diverse climates of the world, through its goodness bestowed on all, incessantly producing joy and activity in every aspect of life, through its unfailing movement, always appearing tranquil, through this constant, unvarying course from which it never deviates, is certainly the most vibrant and magnificent image of a monarch."

Louis XIV and the Grand Dauphin on horseback in front of the Grotto of Thetis, French School, circa 1673.

The east-west axis is thus emphasised by the Fountain of Latona protecting her children Diana and Apollo from the wrath of the Lycian peasants; sunflower vases punctuate the Royal Avenue up to the Fountain of Apollo, where the god rises out of the waves to begin his daily course (the sun rises in the west at Versailles!). The resting Apollo, depicted by the magnificent marble group by Girardon and Regnaudin, originally situated in the Grotto of Thetis (on the site of the current lower vestibule of the chapel), has been the main feature of the Grove of the Baths of Apollo since 1776. To the north, where the décor specifically follows the theme of the marine world relative to Tethys, wife of Oceanus and nocturnal hostess of the Sun, Apollo is depicted in the Dragon Fountain, slaying Python the serpent.

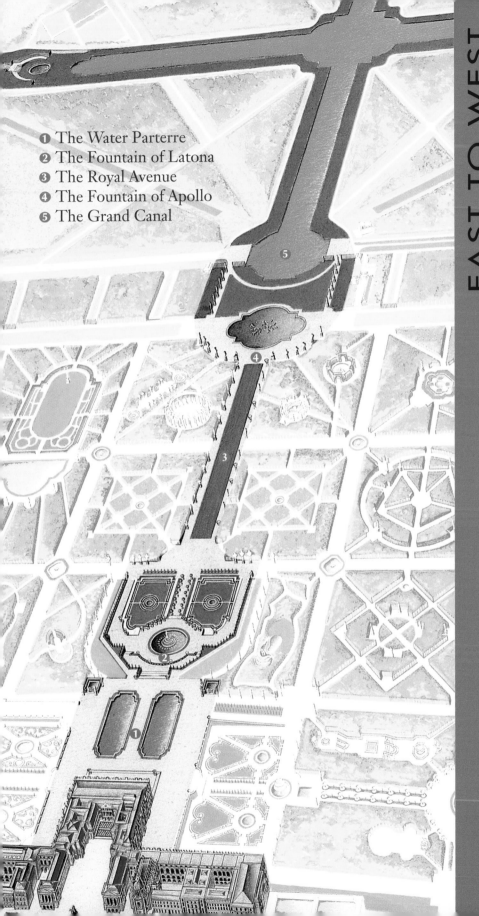

❶ The Water Parterre
❷ The Fountain of Latona
❸ The Royal Avenue
❹ The Fountain of Apollo
❺ The Grand Canal

THE WATER PARTERRE

The two ponds of the Water Parterre, as we see them today, were dug and constructed in 1684-1685; they are represented in their final state following four successive alterations since the reign of Louis XIII. The white marble edges of the ponds are adorned with sixteen bronze statues depicting the rivers and streams of France, cast by the Keller brothers between 1685 and 1694. Following the allegories of classical antiquity, the rivers are depicted by male figures and the streams by female figures. Eight nymphs make up the group.

Air, by
Le Hongre

It is impossible to separate the two Animal Groups, which border the stairway descending towards the Fountain of Latona, from the Water Parterre. Groups of animals cast in bronze by the Keller brothers stand opposite each other on the upper coping. The Animal Group located to the south is also known as the Fountain of Daybreak, and that located to the north, the Fountain of Evening.

The Saône, by Tuby,
The Marne, by Le Hongre,
The Garonne, by Coysevox,
below:
The Seine, by Le Hongre,
right page:
The Loire, by Regnaudin.

From the Water Parterre, a majestic stairway, bordered by two gently sloping inclines forming a crescent, leads to the Fountain of Latona and the two Lizard Fountains. The east-west axis, designed by Le Nôtre, was constructed between 1663 and 1666, at the cost of considerable excavation work. Between 1668 and 1670, the Gaspard brothers and Balthazar Marsy carved the marble figure of Latona holding her children, Apollo and Diana, imploring Jupiter, their father, to avenge the ridicule of the Lycian peasants, who are depicted as being turned into frogs, lizards and tortoises, by the wrath of the god, and are cast in gilded lead. The Fountain of Latona was altered between 1687 and 1689, by Jules Hardouin-Mansart who gave it its current pyramidal form. The statue of Latona looking towards the château, was thus rotated 180 degrees to face the grand perspective of the Royal Avenue.

The Lycian peasants turning into frogs, by the Marsy brothers.

Apollo's Childhood

Juno (the wife of Jupiter), jealous of Latona for bearing her husband's children, exercised her power and banished the expectant mother from every place. After having found her sole refuge to give birth to Apollo and Diana on a bleak rock in the middle of the sea (which then turned into a fertile island and became known as Delos), Latona was forced to resume her wandering. One day, the exhausted Latona, who wanted to bathe her children and drink from the pure spring water in the province of Lycia, was driven out and insulted by peasants inspired by Juno. Enraged, Latona cried out to Jupiter, who turned them into frogs.

This extract from *The Loves of Psyche and Cupid* by La Fontaine evokes the two lizard fountains:

"Two parterres then hold the view;
Both have their fine, fresh grassy rosettes;
Both have a fountain with sparkling treasures,
Feathery plumes in the centre, and arcs along the edges.
Waves surging from the throats of different reptiles;
Hissing lizards, descendants of crocodiles;
And many a tortoise carrying its house,
Stretches out its neck in vain, to escape from prison."

THE CHOICE OF SCULPTURES

In addition to the programmes devised by Charles Le Brun, and the decisions taken directly by Louis XIV, the *Petite Académie* (later the *Académie des Inscriptions*) was responsible for choosing the sculptures and deciding where to place them in the gardens. The *Petite Académie* originated in the group of scholars formed by Colbert in 1663. The institution consisted of four members of the French Academy chosen by the King, and was in charge of supervising everything relating to the celebration of the reign of Louis XIV, with regard to painting, sculpture and tapestry. It had to ensure that the buildings and works of art inspired by Greek or Roman tradition followed the models of classical antiquity. It devised the inscriptions and captions for figures illustrating the great deeds accomplished during the reign of the King.

Barbarian prisoner, by Lespagnandelle.

Above, left to right: Belvedere Antinous, by Legros. Mercury, by Mélo. Callipygian Venus, by Clérion.

THE ROYAL AVENUE

Faun with kid,
by Flamen.
Below:
Dying Gaul,
by Mosnier.

The outline of the Royal Avenue goes back to the origin of the garden under Louis XIII. In 1667, Le Nôtre set about enlarging it and, in 1680, had the centre of the avenue grassed. This large strip of grass became known as the *"Tapis Vert"*. 330 metres long and 40 metres wide, the Royal Avenue is adorned with twelve statues and twelve white marble vases, created between 1684 and 1689.

Performance of La Princesse d'Élide,
comic ballet by Molière and Lully, May 6, 1664;
the Royal Avenue serves as the scenery.

GRAND CANAL

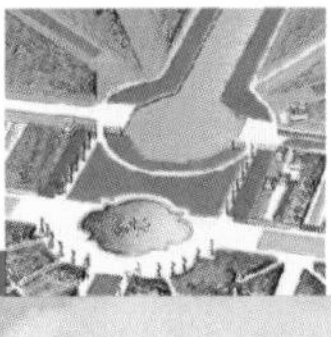

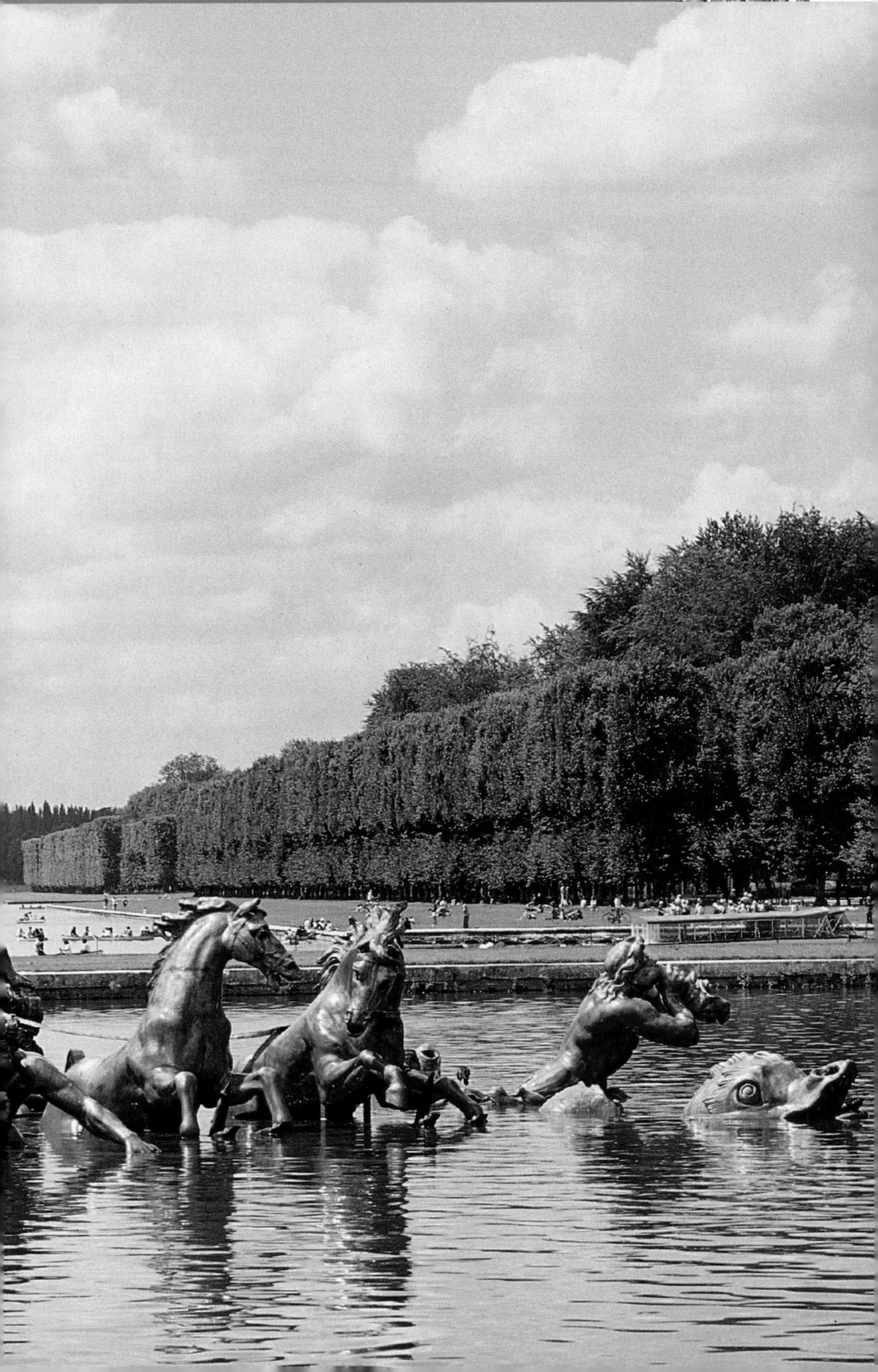

THE FOUNTAIN OF APOLLO

In one of the first maps of Versailles, drawn in 1662, a rectangular quadrilobate pond (then known as Swan Pond), the same size as the current Fountain of Apollo, could be observed at the end of the great east-west avenue. The fountain was constructed on the site of the former circular pond dug in 1636, during the reign of Louis XIII. The lead sculpture, from which the fountain took its name, showing Apollo in his chariot drawn by four horses, surrounded by four Tritons and four sea monsters, was executed by Tuby in 1668. The sculpture was brought to Versailles from the Gobelins works in 1670, and was gilded and in-

stalled the following year. The work of P. Francastel emphasised the different sources that had inspired Tuby, the Italian sculptor who immigrated to France, to create his masterpiece: the *Aurora* fresco from the Rospigliosi collection, painted by Guido Reni, and the statue of *Ares Ludovisi*.

André Le Nôtre, by Carlo Maratta.

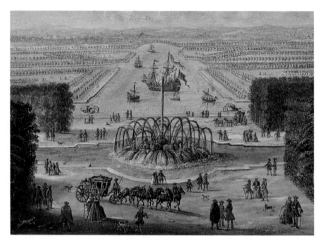

The Fountain of Apollo and the Grand Canal with its flotilla, early 18th century.

THE MYTH OF APOLLO

Apollo, son of Jupiter and Latona, and brother of Diana, is the god of light: both life-giving and fearsome light. He strikes down proud mortals and the tutelary demons of the ancient cults. God of intelligence, reason, music and poetry, he is the protector of world harmony. However, the sun also represents the passing of time, hence the variations on the theme illustrated by the twenty-four statues from the Great Commission of 1674.

The Fountain of Apollo and the Grand Canal in 1713, by Pierre-Denis Martin. In the foreground, Louis XIV out walking.

Digging of the Grand Canal commenced in 1668, and the transverse stretch, which joins the menagerie at Trianon, was initiated in 1671. The construction work continued until 1679. In 1669, before the work was completed, the King had ships and boats sent from Marseilles and Le Havre to sail on the canal. In 1674, four gondoliers and two gondolas arrived from Venice.

"The 10th (January 1751), owing to a glorious frost, I went out alone, in my frock coat, unknown, onto the canal, which had completely frozen over, and thoroughly amused myself for two hours on the ice, watching the skaters. I learned that the good skaters could cover two lengths of the canal, which measures eight hundred fathoms, in six minutes, which would make six and a third leagues in one hour. I was pushed along in a charming sleigh, from one end to the other, and tried my hand at skating, which I managed easily, holding myself up by pushing the sleigh. This is a superb view of the canal covered with people and seen from above. In the evening, I returned for supper in Paris."
Journal of the Duc de Cröy

The Grand Canal flotilla at the end of the reign of Louis XIV.

THE GRAND CANAL FLOTILLA

At the top of the Grand Canal, on the northern side, there remains a cluster of small buildings which, during the 17th century, belonged to what was known as Little Venice. This is where the Venetians sent by the Venetian Republic to row the gondolas given to the King lived from 1674, along with the sailors, ship-

wrights and boatswains responsible for the upkeep of the Grand Canal flotilla. In addition to the gondolas, the flotilla included several ships which were scaled-down versions (the draught being a maximum of 1 metre) of French models built in the naval dockyard: small boats, rowing boats, galleys, and frigates etc., and foreign models: an English yacht and a Dutch barge were brought to Versailles in 1675. At the end of the reign of Louis XIV, more than twenty craft were anchored on the Grand Canal. The royal galley, blue decorated with gold, almost 20 m long, was steered by 42 rowers. The rowing boats, of different sizes, built and decorated according to designs by Philippe Caffieri, were the preferred vessels for royal outings: at the centre, a coach (or chamber) richly hung with varying shades of damask, from which the boat took its name, was furnished with comfortable seats and carpets, painstakingly de-scribed in the Crown Furniture Inventory. Thus, the King was able to judge on actual evidence the progress made by his navy, developed by Colbert, Seignelay, and Pontchartrain.

Northern stretch of the Grand Canal with the Grand Trianon in the background, by Louis-Nicolas de Lespinasse in 1780.

VERSAILLES, A MARITIME PORT

The permanent, vast construction site imposed by the work carried out on the gardens of Versailles was not unrelated to the major projects undertaken throughout France in order to improve communication routes, navigable routes in particular. The most outstanding accomplishment was the *Canal des Deux Mers*, more widely known today as the *Canal du Midi*, which links the Atlantic to the Mediterranean. Its creator, engineer Pierre Paul Riquet had also envisaged a link between the Loire and the Grand Canal, and this project would have thus enabled Versailles to be connected, via a system of canals, to all of the seas surrounding France.

The Grand Canal Flotilla, early 20th century.

The Mercure Galant *of February 1681, informed its readers that "there are shipwrights at Versailles building a new design of frigate, similar to the English frigate but more refined, so it is claimed, as regards both the masts and the trim, which will be designed to carry the sails and remain buoyant despite being heavily loaded with artillery. The frigate, which should only have a 30-foot keel, will nevertheless be able to carry 60 cannons. Monsieur Le Chevalier de Tourville is in charge of the work. If, when accomplished, the design fulfils its promises, all future frigates will be built on this model." When the reign of the King came to an end, the flotilla was left to ruin. During the 18th century, only rowing boats and gondolas continued to sail on the Grand Canal for leisurely outings.*

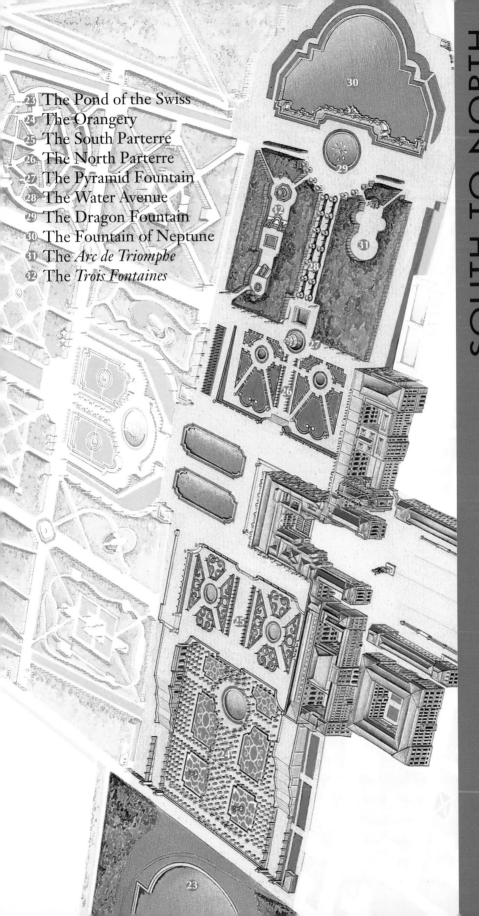

THE SOUTH PARTERRE

Until 1688, the South Parterre was known as the Parterre of Love, or the Queen's Parterre. Situated beneath the windows of the Queen's apartment, which provided the best view, the parterre consists of box edging which originally stood out on a background of coloured stones. It attained its current shape and size after the Orangery was built by Jules Hardouin-Mansart and completed in 1688. Situated slightly below the Water Parterre, it is reached via a few steps flanked by *Children Riding on a Sphinx* replicas of Sarazin's model, created by Lerambert and Houzeau in 1667. The northern part of the marble coping bordering the South Parterre is adorned with bronze vases from a design by Ballin in 1665, cast by Duval. The bronze vases to the east and west are replicas cast by Calla in 1852."

The central body of the château. View from the South Parterre.

VISITING THE GARDENS

From its very creation, visitors came in their multitudes to Versailles. Louis XIV wanted to make the royal residence a genuine showcase for France. Besides the courtiers who had permanent access to the gardens and, depending on their status, were permitted to enter the most prestigious places, all manner of people would crowd in to admire the gardens, already famous throughout the whole of Europe. The gardens were open to the public, even though access was governed by frequently changing regulations. According to Dangeau, on April 13, 1685: "The King, no longer able to walk in his gardens without being overwhelmed by the multitude of people who came from all directions, especially Paris, ordered the guards to allow only members of the Court and their guests to enter. The riffraff visiting the gardens had ruined many of the statues and vases." The first visitor's guide dating from 1674, and written by André Félibien met with great success and was reprinted several times. The foreword proves that there were already many visitors since the authors specified: "... the house is visited every day by people from the whole of France, and foreigners delight in listening to its wondrous tales..."

Sleeping Ariadne,
by Van Clève,
in the style of classical antiquity.
Below:
Children Riding on a Sphinx,
by Lerambert and Houzeau,
after Sarazin.

The two parallel 100-step stairways lead from the South Parterre down to the Orangery Parterre. The present Orangery, built by Hardouin-Mansart between 1681 and 1688, replaced Le Vau's brick and stone building constructed in 1663, which was half the size. The new Orangery is made up of three aisles, two beneath the 100-step stairways, 110 m in length, and the third, facing south, 156 m long, 11.90 m wide and 13 m high (beneath the vault). The thick walls (5 m), and double-glazed windows and doors stabilise the temperature at between 5 and 8°C in winter. The Orangery currently houses 1055 trees planted in boxes (wooden boxes with a frame based on the model used in the 17th century), listed as follows: 690 citrus trees (21 varieties), 170 palm trees (7 varieties), 80 oleanders (13 varieties), 63 pomegranate trees (5 varieties) and 52 Eugenia trees (2 varieties).

The trees are taken out onto the Orangery Parterre between mid-May and mid-October. They are now the sole decorative feature of this large 3-hectare parterre which was restored in 2001 according to a design by Le Nôtre dating from the end of the 17th century, and consists of separate lawned areas with a boxwood border divided into six main compartments. Two gates lead to the Pond of the Swiss, over the road from Versailles to Saint-Cyr.

The Pond of the Swiss

The Pond of the Swiss is 682 m long and 234 m wide. Its surface area (16 ha) is twice the size of the Place de la Concorde in Paris.

The Pond of the Swiss, begun in 1678 and completed in 1688, is flanked east and west by two tree-lined avenues. The work, partly carried out by the regiment of the Swiss Guard, hence its name, made it possible to drain this marshy part of the Great Park where the *Étang Puant* was to be found, and more easily reach the kitchen garden, created between 1678 and 1683, according to plans by La Quintynie, who had already been entrusted with the care of the orange trees. Measuring over 9 hectares, the famous kitchen garden opened onto the avenue running along the eastern side the Pond of the Swiss, through the magnificent King's gate, created by Alexis Fordrin in 1683. The equestrian statue of Louis XIV by Bernini, transformed by Girardon into Marcus Curtius, was placed at the southernmost end of the Pond of the Swiss in 1702.

VUË DU CHATEAU DE VERSAILLES
du coté de la Piece d'Eau des Suisses.

THE NORTH PARTERRE

From the château terrace, the North Parterre is reached via a white marble stairway flanked by two statues: *Chaste Venus* and the *Knife-Grinder*. In 1873, *Chaste Venus*, Coysevox' replica (1684-1686) of an antique model from the Villa Borghese, and the *Knife-Grinder* G.-B. Foggini's replica in 1684 after a Florence antique, were moved to the Louvre to be replaced by two bronzes, on the same subject, cast in 1688 by the Keller brothers and Vinache. The North Parterre is made up of large triangular, slightly raised grassy areas surrounded by trimmed box tree hedges. These box tree borders also demarcate the numerous flower-beds. On each side of the central avenue, the two circular ponds,

known as the Crown Ponds, are the work of Le Hongre and Tuby (1669). Each pond comprises swimming mermaids and tritons, which once held a fleur-de-lys crown.

Right:
Chaste Venus,
after Coysevox.

THE GARDENS OF VERSAILLES, A SCIENCE LABORATORY

Some of the most prominent scientists of the 17th century lent their support to the construction of the gardens of Versailles. Such was the case for Abbé Picard, astronomer and founder of geodesy: a science studying the size, shape and gravitational field of the earth, who by inventing the topographical telescope level enabled the differences in terrain to be accurately measured. This in itself helped to control the different heights of the water jets. One can also mention Philippe de la Hire, astronomer and physician who contributed to the first regular meteorological observations, and who was called on to solve the problem of the water supply to Versailles.

THE PYRAMID FOUNTAIN

Girardon's Pyramid Fountain is situated below the central avenue of the North Parterre. Created according to a design by the painter Le Brun, installation of the fountain began in 1669 and was completed in 1672. The various sculptures are made of lead. The Pyramid is made up of four marble bowls placed one on top the other, in decreasing size. Four large tritons with two tails swimming in the circular pond support the lower bowl in which rest four young tritons supporting the second smaller bowl. The third bowl is supported by the tails of four dolphins in the second bowl. Lastly, four crayfish are buttressed between this and the upper bowl crowned with an urn, from which foaming water springs forth.

At the top of the Water Avenue is the Cascade usually referred to as the Bathing Nymphs. It collects water running down from the Pyramid Fountain situated above. The south supporting wall is adorned with a large lead bas-relief, which was once gilded, by Girardon (1668-1670), depicting nymphs bathing and playing by the side of a river. Le Gros, Le Hongre and Magnier designed the bas-reliefs on the walls at right-angles, depicting nymphs, personifications of rivers, young children and aquatic creatures.

THE WATER AVENUE

The Water Avenue, familiarly known as the *Allée des Marmousets*, leads down a gentle slope from the Bathing Nymphs to the Dragon Fountain. It was undoubtedly devised by Claude Perrault, if we are to believe his brother Charles: "My brother also did the designs for the Water Avenue, which were completely executed." The avenue is split into three sections by two grassy strips, with seven fountains on each one. In their initial state, the small fountains,

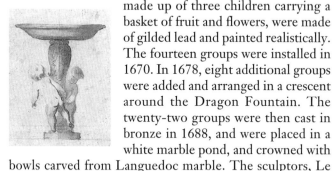

made up of three children carrying a basket of fruit and flowers, were made of gilded lead and painted realistically. The fourteen groups were installed in 1670. In 1678, eight additional groups were added and arranged in a crescent around the Dragon Fountain. The twenty-two groups were then cast in bronze in 1688, and were placed in a white marble pond, and crowned with bowls carved from Languedoc marble. The sculptors, Le Gros, Le Hongre, Lerambert, Mazeline and Buirette, modelled the figures according to Le Brun's designs.

Three little boys, by Buirette. Left and below: Designs for two "children" fountains, by L'Agence des Bâtiments du Roi, circa 1668.

The Dragon Fountain

The Dragon Fountain, which appeared on a map in 1663, was adorned with a lead sculpture by the Marsy brothers in 1667. The two sculptors depicted an episode from the legend of Apollo: Python, the serpent, encircled by dolphins and cupids armed with bows and arrows, riding on swans. This loathsome dragon, son of Gaea (earth goddess), was the tutelary demon of the ancient cults dedicated to the divinities existing before Zeus and the Olympians. Apollo slew the monster with a single arrow. The sculptures were completely restored in 1889, to celebrate the centenary of the opening of the States General at Versailles, and there are almost no remains of the original work. The water jet shooting out of the dragon's mouth, reaching 27 metres, is the highest in the gardens.

THE FOUNTAIN OF NEPTUNE

The Fountain of Neptune forms a group at the northern end of the park, which took almost a century to create. From 1678, Le Nôtre envisaged the semi-circular form of the Fountain of Neptune, then known as the pond "below the Dragon", or the "*Pièce des Sapins*". It was built between 1679 and 1684, under the supervision of first Le Nôtre and then J. Hardouin-Mansart. In 1684, the bowls and shells came to adorn the supporting wall, on the upper rim of which stood twenty-two gilded lead vases. The twenty-two water jets in the channel, the twenty-two jets shooting out of the vases, and the six sprays shooting upwards from the front of the fountain would play for the first time before Louis XIV on May 17, 1685. However, financial difficulties at the end of his reign prevented the completion of this magnificent hydraulic group. It had to be almost completely rebuilt by the architect, Gabriel, between 1733 and 1738, mainly straightening the supporting wall and slightly modifying the dimensions.

Illumination of the Grandes-Eaux in the Fountain of Neptune during the festivities ordered by Napoleon III for the King of Spain, Don François, on August 21, 1864.

Neptune and Amphitrite,
by Lambert-Sigisbert Adam
(1740).

In 1735, the Superintendent of the King's Buildings organised a competition to decorate the fountain. The winner was Lambert-Sigisbert Adam, who executed the central group representing Neptune and Amphitrite in 1740. In 1739, E. Bouchardon modelled the lead figure of Proteus riding on a sea unicorn to the left. To the right of the central group is the god Oceanus, leaning on a conch carried by fish, the work of J.-B. Lemoyne (1740). To the east and west of the fountain are two cupids astride two giant dragons, the work of Bouchardon. This fountain, as we see it today, was inaugurated by Louis XV on August 14, 1741. There are 99 water effects in total.

THE ARC DE TRIOMPHE

The *Bosquet de l'Arc de Triomphe*, created between 1677 and 1684, like its symmetrical counterpart the *Bosquet des Trois Fontaines*, demonstrates the close collaboration between Le Nôtre and the Francine brothers, the King's fountain-makers, in charge of realising all of the water effects dreamed up by the landscape designer. Water did not simply flow through the gardens, it gushed forth, bubbled up, created optical illusions, took on the appearance of crystal, and took every possible form. The grove was closed in 1787 and destroyed in 1801. The Triumphant France sculptural group was restored and returned to the fountain in 2001

The Bosquet de l'Arc de Triomphe by Jean Cotelle.
Centre: Statue of Triumphant Fran by Tuby, Coysevox and Prou.

THE TROIS FONTAINES

Depicted here by Jean Cotelle in 1688, the *Bosquet des Trois Fontaines* replaced the *Berceau d'Eau* in 1677. Jets of water formed a tunnel through which one could walk without getting wet. There were no sculptures in the *Bosquet des Trois Fontaines*, which was more varied in terms of hydraulic motifs, thus displaying its supreme mastery of natural elements. This grove, which disappeared in 1804, is currently being restored.

THE DIFFERENT WORKERS

Upkeep of the gardens necessitated the involvement of several guilds, especially due to the highly organised division of labour. In the gardens one would therefore see woodcutters, curriers, people carrying hay to the cold-stores, and mole catchers... The Liard family, who had the monopoly on mole catching, exterminated almost 6000 moles during the first six months of 1678!

6 The Fountain of Bacchus
7 The Fountain of Saturn
8 The Queen's Grove
9 The Bosquet de Rocailles
10 The Candelabra Grove
11 The King's Garden
12 The Colonnade
13 The Salle des Marronniers

THE AVENUE OF BACCHUS AND SATURN

The four Fountains of the Seasons are situated at the crossroads formed by the four main avenues of the park. The Fountains of Flora and Ceres are situated on the northern side of the Royal Avenue, and the Fountains of Saturn and Bacchus, on the southern side. They were executed according to Le Brun's designs, from 1672. The sculptures were made of lead; the figures were once gilded and the accessories painted realistically.

The Fountain of Saturn or Winter (1675-1677), by Girardon. The ageing, melancholic Saturn is lying on a rock covered with icicles, seaweed and shells.

"From Time, his great wings spread, and deep lines of the years (...) on his lips the bitter expression of the gods, who wish to die but must live forever." (Pierre de Nolhac).

The Fountain of Bacchus or Autumn (1673-1675). The Marsy brothers depicted the god crowned with vines. He is surrounded by little satyrs lying on a sumptuous harvest, with bunches of grapes showing on the surface of the water.

In 1775-1776, the Queen's Grove replaced the Maze Grove created in 1669, based on an idea by Charles Perrault. It was decorated with 39 realistically painted lead fountains

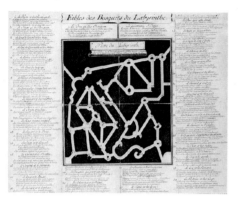

depicting the animals in Aesop's Fables. Due to the fragility of the décor and the decision to replant the gardens, the grove was destroyed and a new "modern" garden created. Rare trees were planted: Virginia tulip trees, Corsican pine trees, etc. and two magnificent cedars of Lebanon, undoubtedly planted in 1775 (one of which fell during the storm in February 1992; this cedar, 35 m tall, had been planted by order of Louis XV towards 1760, in the botanical gardens of Trianon, and then transplanted here in 1775). It was in this grove in 1784, that one of the first chapters of *L'Affaire du Collier de la Reine* unfolded. The present sculptures were installed at the end of the 19th century.

> Among the almost infinite marvels of the magnificent and beautiful House of Versailles, the Maze is one which, perhaps not extremely breathtaking at first sight, but after some consideration, undoubtedly has more charm than any other. It is a square of young, strong trees forming a thick dense wood, intersected with numerous paths which merge into each other so ingeniously that there is nothing more pleasurable than to lose one's way in it.
>
> Charles Perrault (1675)

Top:
Map of
the Maze Grove,
17th century.

Centre:
One of the
sculptures from
the Maze:
the Wolf and
the Head,
by Le Hongre.

Opposite:
Medici Venus,
bronze cast
by the Keller
brothers.

This grove used to be known as the Ballroom "because of the arena in which one may dance when it so pleases His Majesty to hold some celebration there". Construction of the grove, one of Le Nôtre's rare creations that still remains intact, commenced in 1680, and was completed in 1685. The incline of the terrain in this part of the park made it possible for Le Nôtre to build a cascade, the steps of which were adorned with millstones and shells brought from the Red Sea and the Indian Ocean by the royal navy. Opposite the small cascades, an amphitheatre with grass-covered steps would enable spectators to sit and admire the dancers swirling around the centre of the arena, the layout of which had been modified several times. The musicians would be seated above the cascade.

Lead basin covered in shells.

The north-western exit of the Ballroom, at the foot of the Latona incline, opened onto the entrance to the former Candelabra Grove (South Quincunxes). The Candelabra Grove, like its symmetrical counterpart in the northern part of the park, the Dauphin's Grove (today the North Quincunxes), appears on the first maps of Versailles showing the state of the park in 1663, after the initial work carried out by Le Nôtre.

The two groves, which were replanted in quincunx form in 1775-1776, have just been restored to their original state at the end of the reign of Louis XIV, by P.-A. Lablaude (1999-2000).

Eleven of the sixteen terms decorating the two groves were carved after models by Poussin, commissioned by Superintendent Fouquet in 1655. These terms, which adorned the gardens of Vaux-Le-Vicomte, were purchased by the King in 1683, and then brought to the gardens of Versailles.

Top:
Ceres,
by Théodon
(the Dauphin's Grove).

Left:
Reaper holding a sickle,
by Théodon
(The Candelabra Grove).

Opposite:
Pomona,
by Théodon
(The Candelabra Grove).

THE KING'S GARDEN

Not far from the Queen's Grove, the King's Garden is on the site of the Royal Island, a large pond dug between 1671 and 1674, to drain this marshy part of the gardens. To the east of the pond, on the other side of the Avenue of Saturn, another pond was dug, the Mirror Pond, surrounded by a shelf, water from which flowed into the Royal Island. Only the Mirror Pond remains today. Since the park was virtually left to ruin during the Revolution and Empire periods, the Royal Island pond disappeared. Embankment work was carried out during the winter of 1816-1817. Alexandre Dufour, architect of the châteaux of Versailles from 1810 to 1832, created the King's Garden on this very site, in the picturesque style of an English garden, greatly prized at the time. It is planted with more than one hundred and fifty trees and shrubs, complemented by flower-beds comprising 50 different species, thus representing a superb botanical collection.

TREES FROM ELSEWHERE

Large diameter trees were often imported to be planted in the gardens. In 1671, yew trees were brought from the forests of Normandy, and in 1680, other species arrived from Compiègne. Elm and lime trees were brought from Flanders, and spruces from the Dauphiné mountains. In 1688, 25,000 trees were purchased in Artois. Madame de Sévigné could thus marvel at these "sturdy, dense forests being brought to Versailles."

THE COLONNADE

In 1679, close to the *Galerie d'Eau*, in this lower, marshy part of the park, Le Nôtre created the Grove of Springs: narrow winding paths wove their way through the wood, crossing several little streams. The Grove of Springs had a very short existence: on June 19, 1684, "the King commissioned a marble colonnade with large fountains on the very site of the Springs" (Extract from the Journal kept by Marquis Dangeau).

The Colonnade, construction of which commenced in 1685, with its extremely marked architectural design, devoid of all plant life, is the work J. Hardouin-Mansart. The perfect circular peristyle measures 32 m in diameter. 32 marble columns, of the Ionic order, of purple breccia, Languedoc marble, or slate-blue marble, coupled to 32 Languedoc marble pilasters, support the archways and a white marble cornice upon which are

32 urns. The triangular spandrels between the archways are decorated with bas-reliefs mainly depicting children playing musical instruments, evocative of the purpose of the grove which was the setting for numerous concerts. The stones forming the curved parts of the arches are adorned with the heads of nymphs and naiads etc. The sculptures are the work of Coysevox, Tuby, Le Hongre, Le Conte, Mazière and Granier etc. Fountains in the form of large marble basins are under each archway, water from which flows into a channel.

In 1699, Louis XIV had the group executed by Girardon (1677-1699), originally intended for the third water parterre, placed at the centre of the Colonnade: The Rape of Persephone by Pluto has been placed on a pedestal decorated with a bas-relief illustrating the story of the abduction of Ceres' daughter.

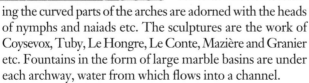

THE SALLE DES MARRONNIERS

In 1704, the *Salle des Marronniers* replaced the *Salle des Antiques* or *Galérie d'Eau*, arranged by Le Nôtre from 1680. In 1683, twenty-four classical statues were installed there on pedestals placed in a little water channel encircling the long, narrow island. The ends of the gallery were adorned with two fountains.

Jules Hardouin-Mansart retained the long, narrow form of the old grove, which can still be seen today, and was described by Piganiol in 1717: "The *Salle des Marronniers* (Chestnut Hall) was thus named since the wings which were once made up of water jets and statues now consist of chestnut trees. The fences are decorated with eight white marble classical busts [...], there are also two classical statues of white marble representing Antinous and Meleager".

THE FRENCH ACADEMY IN ROME

The French Academy in Rome was founded by Colbert in 1666. The sculptors in residence were responsible for casting and copying classical statues for the King. Hence, in 1679, 300 cases of sculptures were sent from Rome. The absolute nudity of the figures clearly shocked the prudes at Versailles since a sculptor was commissioned, in 1687, to carve "leaves to cover the nakedness of the figures in the gardens."

Top:
Antinous,
French School
of the 17th century
(after classical antiquity).

Opposite:
Meleager,
French School
of the 17th century
(after classical antiquity).

THE AVENUE OF FLORA AND CERES

The Fountain of Flora or Spring (1672-1675) is circular in form. It was created by Tuby. The semi-naked goddess is resting on a bed of flowers, surrounded by young cupids amusing themselves weaving garlands which "become entangled and fall into the pool... Tuby imagined her almost naked...; her hand rests on a basket brimming over with cornflowers, anemones, every type of old French flower" (P. de Nolhac).

The Fountain of Ceres or Summer (1672-1674) is octagonal in form. This group, created by Regnaudin, depicts the goddess holding a sickle. Around her, naked cupids lie on the ground strewn with ears of wheat. "This work is only complete (...) under the jet of water which falls in showers (...) on the scattered harvest mingled with wild flowers. Ceres is leaning back surrounded by her offerings, blissfully watching the column of water shooting up towards the foliage" (P. de Nolhac) and streaming onto the pedestal and the three cupids frolicking around her.

THE FESTIVITIES OF 1668

In 1668, Louis XIV celebrated his recent military victories concerning the conquest of Flanders. Carlo Vigarani built a theatre which could hold one thousand two hundred spectators on the site where the Fountain of Bacchus was to be installed, for the performance of Les Fêtes de l'Amour et de Bacchus by Molière and Lully. On the site of the present Fountain of Flora, decorator Henri de Gissey and fountain-maker François Francine devised a temporary pavilion where approximately four hundred and fifty guests came to dine. A sumptuous ballroom, created by Le Vau, was also built on the site where the Fountain of Ceres eventually stood.

THE FOUNTAIN OF ENCELADUS

The Fountain of Enceladus was created by Le Nôtre in 1675. The subject was taken from the overthrow of the Titans crushed by rocks of Mount Olympus as they were climbing in defiance of Zeus. The grove was reworked by Hardouin-Mansart in 1706, who kept only the central fountain decorated with a figure of Enceladus, the giant, in gilded lead, the work of Gaspard Marsy. The grove was restored according to Le Nôtre's designs between 1992 and 1998.

Galatea,
by Tuby.

THE BOSQUET DES DÔMES

Created by Le Nôtre in 1675, this grove, known as the Grove of Fame (from Marsy's lead statue placed in the centre of the pool between 1677 and 1684), was decorated with two small marble domed pavilions, adorned with gilded bronze and lead trophies. Although they had given their name to the grove, they were destroyed in 1820. The groups from the Baths of Apollo were placed there between 1684 and 1704. The other statues making up the current décor were installed between 1684 and 1705. The circular balustrade is decorated with 44 bas-reliefs by Girardon, Mazeline and Guérin, representing the coats of arms of the different nations.

The Bosquet des Dômes, also known as the Grove of the Baths of Apollo in 1688, by C. Simoneau Le Jeune.

 ## MOVING AROUND THE GARDENS

As is the case today, the gardens could obviously be seen on foot; however, those who were loath to wear themselves out could also use a "wheeled chair". On May 23, 1704, the *Mercure Galant* reported that "wheeled chairs would wait at the door of Monsieur Le Comte de Toulouse's apartment at the garden end. Wheeled chairs are armchairs in which one may visit the gardens; they are sprung and drawn by a porter. However, since they are pushed by two porters, they may go as fast as one wishes."

THE OBELISK GROVE, THE BOSQUET DE L'ETOILE (STAR GROVE), AND THE ROND VERT

The five groves created by Le Nôtre in the northern part of the park have either disappeared or undergone extensive alterations. In 1671, Le Nôtre began work on the grove known as the Council Chamber or Banqueting Hall. (It was transformed by Mansart in 1704-1705 and then became known as the Obelisk Grove). Various excavation work gave the grove its present form: a central pool decorated with a crown of reeds from which spring 231 jets of water reaching a height of 23 m.

To the west of the Obelisk Grove, the Water Mountain Grove (now known as Star Grove) has retained its overall 1671 form, despite the alterations made in 1705. It consists of a circular avenue bordering a pentagonal avenue from which stem five avenues leading to the centre. A round fountain consisting of a mass of rocks representing a small mountain, from which sprang forth twelve jets of water, was at the centre of this ingenious network of pathways, clearly in the style of Le Nôtre. The clearing and the converging avenues were edged with tall trellising covered with honeysuckle and crowned with coloured earthenware vases.

The Banqueting Hall before 1705.
At the centre of the Banqueting Hall was a rectangular quadrilobate island adorned with four round fountains, surrounded by a narrow channel beyond which were four small circular fountains. Two small swing bridges led to the central island.
In 1680-1681, the eight fountains and channel were decorated with lead cupids taken from the four fountains of the seasons.
In 1705, part of the lead décor was taken to the gardens of Trianon.

There are no remains of the Water Theatre, built between 1671 and 1673, and destroyed in 1750. This grove, which took on the form of a theatre, was adorned with eight lead fountains. One of these, *Child Playing with a Dolphin*, by G. Marsy, was taken to the gardens of Trianon in 1705, and two others, *Children Playing the Lyre* by Le Gros and *Children with Swan* by Tuby, are at the National Gallery in Washington. To the west of the grove, a circular pool was dug in 1710, which became known as the *Children's Island*, featuring gilded lead sculptures created by Jean Hardy. This grove is now generally known as the *Rond-Vert*.

Children's Island, by Jean Hardy.

The Grove of the Baths of Apollo, as it exists today, dates from 1775, corresponding to the replanting of the park of Versailles. It replaced the famous grove built from 1670 to 1672, based on an idea by Madame de Montespan, which was known as *Le Marais*. Jules Hardouin-Mansart created a new grove for the same site, which was to be the setting for the *Horses of the Sun* groups located in the *Bosquet des Dômes* between 1684 and 1705, after

the destruction of the famous Grotto of Thetis. This ensemble, created between 1672 and 1677, consists of three groups: the centre group represents *Apollo Served by Nymphs*, by Girardon and Regnaudin. Marsy created one of the two groups representing the *Horses of the Sun, Groomed by the Tritons*, and the other was the work of Gilles Guérin. The painter Hubert Robert was responsible for the arrangement of the groups in the artificial grotto supported by columns, together with the pond and the cascades.

Replanting the Gardens

By the death of Louis XV (1774), the gardens and the little park had existed for over a century. Many of the trees that had survived the ravages of the recent storms were in a pitiful state. Louis XVI thus decided to replant the park, which began in 1775. Two paintings by Hubert Robert depict the vast work site, which also included alteration of four groves: the Maze became the Queen's Grove, the Grove of the Baths of Apollo was restored in the "English" style, whereas the Dauphin's Grove and the Candelabra Grove became the Quincunxes planted out with chestnut trees. Replantation of the gardens and the park was initiated in 1992 and will continue for twenty or so years.

"Once the trees had been felled, the landscape seemed better, there were views, and all the beautiful marbles in this magnificent garden being exposed all at once, a superb ensemble was uncovered".
Memoirs of the Duc de Cröy.

Hubert Robert, Alteration of the Baths of Apollo, oil on canvas, 1776.

1 THE TERRACE

The terrace comprises four bronze statues cast by the Keller brothers from classical works, in 1684-1685.

1. Bacchus at rest
2. Belvedere Apollo
3. Belvedere Antinous
4. Silenus holding Bacchus
   Situated below the Peace and War Drawing-Rooms, respectively:
5. Peace vase, by Tuby, 1684-1685
6. War vase, by Coysevox, 1684-1685

13. The Rhône, by Tuby
14. The Saône, by Tuby
15. Group of Children, by Laviron and Le Gros
16. Nymph, by Raon
17. Nymph, by Raon
18. Group of Children, by Poultier

NORTHERN POND

19. The Garonne, by Coysevox
20. The Dordogne, by Coysevox
21. Group of Children, by Dugoulon
22. Nymph, by Le Gros
23. Nymph, by Le Gros
24. Group of Children, by Granier

43

3 THE ANIMAL GROUPS

FOUNTAIN OF EVENING

31. Air, by Le Hongre, 1685
32. Evening, by Desjardins, 1680
33. Noon, by G. Marsy, 1680 (modern cast of original in reserve)
34. Fighting animals: lion bringing down a boar, and lion bringing down a wolf, bronzes, by Van Clève and Raon, 1687

FOUNTAIN OF DAYBREAK

35. Daybreak, by G. Marsy, 1680
36. Spring, by Magnier, 1681
37. Water, by Le Gros, 1681
38. Fighting animals: tiger bringing down a bear, and bloodhound killing a stag, bronzes, by Houzeau, 1687.
    Numbers 31, 32, 33, 35, 36 and 37 were part of the Great Commission of 1674

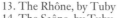

5

2 THE WATER PARTERRE

SOUTHERN POND

7. The Loiret, by Regnaudin
8. The Loire, by Regnaudin
9. Group of Children, by Lespingola
10. Nymph, by Le Hongre
11. Nymph, by Le Hongre
12. Group of Children, by Mazière

37

38

25. The Marne, by Le Hongre
26. The Seine, by Le Hongre
27. Group of Children, by Buirette and Lespingola
28. Nymph, by Magnier
29. Nymph, by Magnier
30. Group of Children, by Van Clève

32

53

4 THE LATONA INCLINE

SOUTHERN INCLINE

39. Lyrical Poem,
    by Tuby, 1675-1680
40. Fire, by Dossier, 1681
41. Tiridates,
    by André, 1687
42. Callipygian Venus,
    by Clérion, 1686
43. Silenus with the child
    Bacchus, by Mazière, 1684
44. Belvedere Antinous,
    by Le Gros, 1686
45. Farnese Mercury,
    by Mélo, 1685
46. Urania, by Carlier, 1684
47. Belvedere Apollo,
    by Mazeline, 1684

NORTHERN INCLINE

48. Melancholy,
    by La Perdrix, 1680
49. Belvedere Antinous,
    by Lacroix
50. Tigranes,
    by Lespagnandelle, 1687
51. Faun Playing the Flute,
    by Hurtrelle, 1685
52. Medici Bacchus,
    by Granier, 1684-1688
53. Faustina or Ceres,
    by Regnaudin, 1684-1685

56

54

54. Commodus as Hercules,
    by N. Coustou, 1686
55. Urania, by Frémery, 1684
56. Ganymede, by Laviron,
    1684-1685
    Numbers 39, 40 and 48
    were part of the Great
    Commission of 1674

5 THE PARTERRE OF LATONA

STAIRCASE

57. The central avenue
    of the Water Parterre
    leads to the staircase

Flanking the top
of the staircase:
58. Sun vase,
    by Drouilly, 1687
59. Sun vase,
    by Dugoulon, 1687
Overhanging the Fountain
of Latona are four marble
vases, including one
(62 or 63) by Grimault (1673)
and the other three
by students of the French
Academy in Rome.
60. 61. Vases encircled with ivy
    and oak leaves
62. 63. Covered vases
    decorated with vines
    and satyr masks

THE FOUNTAIN OF LATONA

In the water: lead turtles
and lizards surround
the central pyramid

1st tier: semi-metamorphosed
  peasants and frogs
2nd and 3rd tiers: frogs
4th tier: base supporting
  a rock on which stands
  the suppliant Latona
  surrounded by her children
  Apollo and Diana,
  by Balthazar and Gaspard
  Marsy (cast of the marble
  original from 1668-1670,
  in reserve).

TERRACE

64. 66. 68. Borghese vases
    (Bacchanal)
65. Vase depicting
    the childhood of Mars,
    by Prou, 1684
67. 69. 71. Medici vases
    (sacrifice of Iphigenia)
Numbers 67 and 68 by Cornu,
and numbers 64, 66, 69
and 71 by Hurtrelle, Laviron
and Le Conte, 1673 to 1683

67

75

78

79

70. Vase depicting
the childhood of Mars,
by Hardy, 1684
72. 73. Lizard Fountains,
by the Marsy brothers,
1668-1670
In each fountain, two Lycian
peasants metamorphosed
while picking reeds.

6 THE CRESCENT AROUND THE PARTERRE OF LATONA

74. Dying Gladiator,
by Mosnier, circa 1680
75. Circe, by Magnier,
1684-1686
76. Plato, by Rayol, 1685-1688
77. Mercury, by Van Clève,
1684-1687
78. Pandora, by Le Gros,
1685-1686
79. Achelous, by Mazière, 1688
80. Castor and Pollux, group,
by Coysevox, 1685-1712
81. Aria and Poetus, group,
by Lespingola, 1684-1688

80

81

82

87

82. Laocoon and his sons,
group, by Tuby, 1696
83. Peace among the Greeks,
group, by Carlier
and Mosnier, 1685-1688
84. Hercules,
by Le Conte, 1684-1686
85. Bacchante,
by Dedieu, 1684-1685
86. Faun,
by Houzeau, 1684-1687

89

87. Diogenes,
   by Lespagnandelle,
   1685-1688
88. Ceres, by Poultier,
   after Girardon,
   1687-1688
89. Nymph with shell,
   after Coysevox,
   by A. Suchetet, 1891

7 The Candelabra Grove
90. Morpheus, after Poussin
91. Flora, after Poussin
92. Hercules, after Poussin
93. Pomona, after Poussin
94. Reaper, by Théodon
95. Bacchante, by Laviron
96. Vertumnus, after Poussin
97. Minerva, after Poussin

97

107

8 The Dauphin's Grove
98. Flora, by Lacroix
99. Pan, after Poussin
100. Liberality,
    after Poussin
101. Faun, after Poussin
102. Ceres, by Théodon
103. Bacchus,
    after Poussin
104. Plenty, after Poussin
105. Winter, by Théodon

111

9 ROYAL AVENUE
(Length: 330 m, width: 40 m)
   TO THE NORTH
106. Geometric vase,
    diamonds originally
    decorated with fleurs-de-lys,
    by Poultier, 1684-1688
107. Deceit,
    by Le Conte, 1684-1685
108. Juno, classical statue
    discovered at Smyrna
    and restored, by Mazière
109. Vase decorated
    with flowering cornucopia,
    by Barois, 1687-1696
110. Vase with wide fluting,
    decorated with sunflowers,
    by Dugoulon, 1687-1689
111. Hercules and Telephus,
    by Jouvenet, 1684-1685
112. Medici Venus,
    by Mosnier and Frémery,
    1687
113. Sunflower vase, by Arcis
114. Fluted vase with
    acanthus leaves,
    by Vigier, 1687-1688
115. Cyparissus stroking his
    deer, by Flamen, 1687
116. Artemisia,
    by Lefèvre and Desjardins,
    1687-1695

115

117. Vase with oak and laurel
    branches, originally
    decorated with the King's
    monogram, by Lefèvre, 1687
TO THE SOUTH
118. Geometric vase,
    diamonds originally
    decorated with fleurs-de-lys,
    by Herpin, 1687-1688
119. Fidelity, by Lefèvre, 1684
120. Venus rising
    out of the sea, also known
    as the Richelieu Venus,
    by Le Gros, 1685-1689
121. Vase decorated
    with flowering cornucopia,
    by Rayol, 1687-1688
122. Vase with wide fluting,
    decorated with sunflowers,
    by Légeret, 1687-1689

119

69

125

123. Faun with kid,
by Flamen, 1685-1686
124. Dido, by Poultier, 1689
125. Sunflower vase,
by Slodtz, 1687
126. Fluted vase with acanthus
leaves, by Joly, 1687
127. Amazon,
by Buirette, 1685-1693
128. Achilles at Scyros,
by Vigier, 1695
129. Vase with oak and laurel
branches, originally decorated
with the King's monogram,
by Hardy, 1687

10 THE FOUNTAIN
OF APOLLO
Apollo in his chariot,
by Jean-Baptiste Tuby,
1668-1670

128

11 THE CRESCENT
AROUND THE
FOUNTAIN OF APOLLO
TO THE SOUTH
130. Bacchus, classical statue
restored by Duseigneur in 1853
131. Pomona,
by Le Hongre, 1684-1689
132. Bacchus,
by Raon, 1687-1689
133. Spring,
by Arcis and Mazière, 1688
134. The god Pan,
by Mazière, 1686-1689
135. Ino and Melicertes,
by Granier, 1686-1712
TO THE NORTH
136. Aristaeus and Proteus,
by Slodtz

133

137. Syrinx,
by Mazière, 1686-1689
138. Jupiter,
by Clérion, 1686-1689
139. Juno,
by Clérion, 1686-1689
140. Vertumnus,
by Le Hongre, 1684-1689
141. Silenus holding the child
Bacchus, classical statue

12 AVENUES FROM THE
FOUNTAIN OF APOLLO
TO THE GRAND CANAL
TO THE SOUTH
142. Roman figure,
classical statue
143. Bacchus,
by R. Le Lorrain, 1710-1712
144. Farnese Hercules,
classical statue

136

145. Woman with child,
classical statue
146. Hercules, modern statue,
by Grégoire, 1926
147. Juno, after classical
antiquity
TO THE NORTH
148. Roman emperor,
classical statue
149. Bacchus, modern statue,
by Grégoire, 1926
150. Apollo with a lyre,
classical statue
151. Daylight, by Baldi
152. Roman figure,
classical statue
153. Cleopatra,
after classical antiquity

13 THE GRAND CANAL
The Grand Canal is 62 metres
wide and 1650 metres long.
A transverse arm stretches
from the former Menagerie
to the Grand Trianon.

14 THE *BOSQUET DES
DÔMES*
154. Ino, by Rayol, 1686-1688
155. Daybreak,
by Le Gros, 1686-1696
156. Acis, by Tuby, 1667-1672

143

154

155

156

157. Aurora, by Magnier, 1704
158. Galatea, by Tuby,
1667-1672
159. Amphitrite, after Anguier
(modern copy,
original in reserve)
160. Arion with lyre,
by Raon, 1686-1695
161. Nymph of Diana,
by Flamen, 1705
162. Marble vase decorated
with musical instruments
and garlands of flowers,
by Robert, 1688-1689

15 THE FOUNTAIN OF ENCELADUS
163. Enceladus, lead sculpture,
by G. Marsy, 1675-1677

16 THE OBELISK
Formerly the grove
of the Banqueting Hall.
164. Two small curved
pedestals

17 THE FOUNTAIN OF FLORA
165. Flora and four cupids,
lead sculptures,
by J.B. Tuby, 1672-1679

160

18 THE *BOSQUET DE L'ETOILE* (STAR GROVE)
Formerly the Water Mountain
Grove
166. Five empty pedestals
171. Muse with nebris,
classical statue.

165

167

170

19 THE FOUNTAIN OF CERES

172. Ceres and three cupids,
lead sculptures,
by Regnaudin, 1672-1679

20 THE BATHS OF APOLLO

At the centre of the grotto:
167. Group representing Apollo
Served by Nymphs, by Girardon
and Regnaudin, 1666-1672
168. The Horses of the Sun,
Groomed by the Tritons:
group with rearing horse,
by the Marsy brothers
169. Group with horse drinking,
by Guérin, 1664-1666

168

21 THE ROND VERT

(Formerly the grove
of the Water Theatre)
173. Dancing faun (pedestal)
174. Pomona
175. Ganymede, by Joly, 1683
176. Ceres
177. Fountain of the Children's
Island, lead sculptures
by Hardy, 1710
178. Statue in the style of classical
antiquity, known as Cleopatra
179. Hadrian (pedestal)

183

22 THE FOUNTAIN OF NEPTUNE

180. Faustina,
by Frémery, circa 1684
181. The Glory of the King,
by Domenico Guidi,
1680-1685
182. Berenice,
by Lespingola, 1673
183. Cupid riding a sea dragon,
by Bouchardon, 1739

172

Vases, Fountain of Neptune

Water Avenue

184. Proteus leaning on a sea
    unicorn, by Bouchardon, 1739
185. Neptune and Amphitrite,
    by Lambert-Sigisbert Adam,
    1740
186. Oceanus riding sea
    creatures,
    by Jean-Baptiste Lemoine,
    1740
187. Cupid riding
    a sea dragon,
    by Bouchardon, 1739
Twenty-two lead vases
decorated with
aquatic figures adorn
the inner rim
of the channel,
and line the south
supporting wall decorated
with lead masks
and shells
(late 17th century).

23 THE DRAGON
FOUNTAIN
170. Python, the serpent,
    and four children armed
    with bows and arrows, riding
    on swans. Lead sculptures
    by the Marsy brothers (1667),
    restored by Tony Noël
    (1889)

24 THE WATER AVENUE
188. Three little girls,
    by Buirette
189. Three little boys,
    by Buirette
190. Three hunters,
    by Mazeline
191. 192. Three children
    playing with fish,
    by Mazeline
193. Three hunters,
    by Mazeline
194. Three little boys,
    by Buirette
195. Three little girls,
    by Buirette
196. Three terms,
    by Lerambert
197. Three satyrs, by Le Gros
198. Three musicians,
    by Lerambert
199. Boys and girls dancing,
    by Lerambert
200. Cupids and little girl,
    by Le Hongre
201. Three dancers,
    by Le Gros
202. Three tritons, by Le Gros

THE BATHING NYMPHS
203. Square pool, decorated
    on three sides with lead

bas-reliefs by Le Hongre,
Le Gros and Girardon.
Girardon's Nymphs
of Diana Bathing,
1668-1670,
is on the northern wall.

25 THE BOSQUET
DE L'ARC DE TRIOMPHE

26 THE BOSQUET
DES TROIS FONTAINES

27 THE PYRAMID
FOUNTAIN
204. Lead sculptures,
    by Girardon, 1668-1670

28 THE NORTH
PARTERRE
WESTERN AVENUE
205. Europa, by Mazeline,
    1675-1680
206. Africa by Sybraique and
    Cornu, 1675-1682
207. Night, by Raon,
    1675-1680
208. Earth, by Massou,
    1675-1681
209. Pastoral poem,
    by Hérard and Granier,
    1675-1680

215

216. America, by Guérin,
    1675-1678
217. Summer, by Hutinot,
    1675-1679
218. Winter, by Girardon,
    1675-1686
219. Choleric figure,
    by Houzeau, 1675-1680
220. Sanguine figure,
    by Jouvenet, 1675-1680
221. Satirical poem,
    by Buyster, 1674-1679
222. Asia, by Roger,
    1675-1680
    (cast, original in reserve)
223. Sluggish figure,
    by Lespagnandelle,
    1675-1679

224. Epic poem,
    by Drouilly, 1675-1679
Numbers 215 to 224
were part of
the Great Commission
of 1674.
THE LOWER PARTERRE
225. Two marble vases
    decorated with children
    playing (late 17th century)
226. 227. Crown Ponds.
    Lead sculptures
    by Tuby and Le Hongre,
    1669.
228. Marble vase
    with grape motif,
    by Bertin, 1687-1705
229. Two marble vases
    encircled with oak branches,
    by Cornu, 1684

Numbers 205 to 209 were
part of the Great
Commission of 1674.
PHILOSOPHERS CIRCLE
210 Ulysses, by Magnier,
    1684-1688
211. Isocrate, by Granier,
    1685-1688
212. Theophrastus, by
    Hurtrelle, 1686-1688
213. Lysias, by Dedieu,
    1685
214. Apollonius, by Mélo,
    1685-1687
NORTHERN AVENUE
215. Autumn,
    by Regnaudin, 1675-1680

218

221

230. Marble vase with grape
    motif, by Bertin, 1687
RECTILINEAR COPING
Overhanging the wall
bordering the South Parterre.
A. B. Twelve bronze vases,
    after Ballin, cast
    by Calla, 1852
Six models are repeated
symmetrically.
The handles are in the form
of heads of fauns,
cupids, snarling wolves,
mermaids, and pastoral
and sea gods.
231. Two green marble
    Egyptian vases, by Hurtrelle
    and Mazière, 1685
CENTRAL STAIRWAY
232. The Knife-Grinder,
    after Foggini, 1688.
    Cast by the Keller brothers
233. Chaste Venus,
    after Coysevox, 1688
234. Two bronze vases
    decorated with Rhodian suns
    and encircled with
    classical silhouettes
    in medallions,
    after Michel Anguier.
    Cast by Duval (1665-1666)

217   221

The Hundred Steps

235. Marble vase encircled with vine branches, with handles in the form of rams' heads, by Drouilly, 1685

29 THE SOUTH PARTERRE

236. Sleeping Ariadne, by Van Clève, 1684-1688
C. Nine bronze vases, cast by Calla (1852)
237. 238. Marble vases with dolphin-shaped handles, by Bertin, 1687-1705
239. 240. Marble vases, by Tuby and Hulot, 1697
D. Six bronze vases, cast by Duval (17th century)
241. 242. Children Riding on a Sphinx, bronze and marble, by Lerambert and Houzeau, after Sarazin, 1667-1668

E. Six bronze vases, cast by Duval (17th century)
243. 244. Marble vases with handles in the form of fauns' heads, by Bertin, 1687
F. Nine bronze vases, cast by Calla (1852)
245. Marble vase, Sacrifice to Bacchus, by Bertin, 1687-1705
246. Marble vase, Roman funeral, by Bertin, 1687-1705
C. D. E. F. Like the A and B series of the North Parterre, these bronze vases, with handles in the form of young satyrs, cupids, dragons, mermaids, two-faced Janus figures, etc., were made from designs by Claude Ballin, goldsmith to Louis XIV.

30 THE ORANGERY

247. 248. Marble vases decorated with grapes and vine leaves, by Raon and Buirette, 1685-1693

THE HUNDRED STEPS

TO THE EAST
249. Aurora and Cephalus, by Le Gros, 1687

232

273

257

31 THE QUEEN'S GROVE

32 THE *BOSQUET DE ROCAILLES*

(or The Ballroom)
On the upper level
are four gilded lead vases,
by Le Conte.
Positioned by the entrance
are four vases
in gilded lead,
by Le Hongre,
eight gilded lead
candelabra,
by Massou, Jouvenet,
Le Gros and Mazeline.

33 THE FOUNTAIN OF BACCHUS

258

34 THE WATER MIRROR

262. Marble vase with ivy borders, by Drouilly, 1687
263. Draped woman, classical statue
264. Apollo-Pothos, classical statue
265. Half-draped Venus, classical statue
266. Draped woman, classical statue
267. Marble vase with ivy borders, by Mélo, 1687

35 THE KING'S GARDEN

268. Marble vase in honour of Bacchus, by J. Rousselet, 1680-1683
269. Marble vase with funeral motif, by J. Rousselet, 1680-1683
270. Farnese Flora, by Raon, 1684-1685
271. Farnese Hercules, by Cornu, 1684-1688

36 THE FOUNTAIN OF SATURN

272. The ageing, winged Saturn and four cupids, lead sculpture, by Girardon, 1672-1677.

37 THE COLONNADE

273. Girardon's Rape of Persephone by Pluto (cast, the original is in reserve), 1677-1699
274. Marble vase decorated with garlands of flowers and musical instruments, by Robert, 1688-1689

38. THE SALLE DES MARRONNIERS

(Formerly the grove of the Salle des Antiques)
275. Round pool, white marble basin
276. Marcus Aurelius (bust)
277. Otho (bust)
278. Antinous (statue in the style of classical antiquity)
279. Alexander (bust)
280. Apollo (bust)
281. Round pool, white marble basin
282. Antoninus (bust)
283. Septimus Severus (bust)
284. Meleager (statue in the style of classical antiquity)
285. Octavian (bust)
286. Hannibal (bust)

275

Parterre of Latona, northern incline: 56, 55, 54, 53, 52, see page 67.

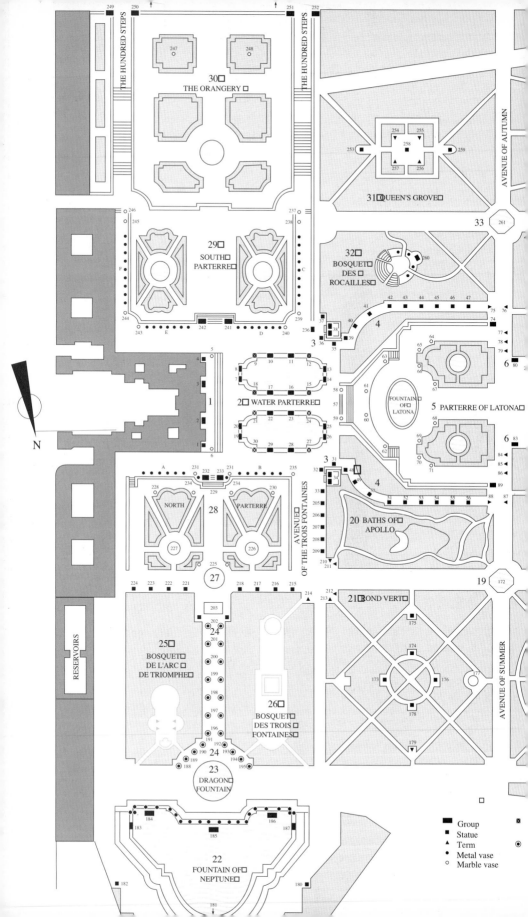

THE HUNDRED STEPS

THE HUNDRED STEPS

249 250 251 252

247 248

30☐
THE ORANGERY ☐

AVENUE OF AUTUMN

254 255
258
257 256
253 259

31☐QUEEN'S GROVE☐

33 261

246 237
245 238

29☐
SOUTH
PARTERRE☐

F C

244 239
243 242 241 240
E D

32☐
BOSQUET
DES ☐
ROCAILLES☐

260

41 42 43 44 45 46 47 75 76
4 74
77
78
79
6 80

3 37 40
36 35 39
38
34

5
9 10 11 12
8 18 13
7 17 16 15 14
58
1

2☐ WATER PARTERRE☐
57

4 3
2
1 6

20 21 22 23 24 25
19 30 29 28 27 26

65 64
66
63 67
61
60
62

68
69
70 71

FOUNTAIN ☐
OF ☐
LATONA

5 PARTERRE OF LATONA☐

6 83
84
85
86

3 31
32
33

49
50

4 51 52 53 54 55 56 88 89 87

205 20 BATHS OF☐
206 APOLLO
207
208
209
210
211

19 172

AVENUE OF THE TROIS FONTAINES

231 232 233 231 235
A 234 229 234 B 230
228 230

NORTH 28 PARTERRE

227 226

27 225

212 21☐ROND VERT☐
213 214

224 223 222 221 218 217 216 215

203

202

25☐
BOSQUET☐
DE L'ARC ☐
DE TRIOMPHE☐

24
201
200
199
198
197
196
191 192
190 193
189 194
188 195
24

175

174

173 176
177
178

AVENUE OF SUMMER

26☐
BOSQUET☐
DES TROIS ☐
FONTAINES☐

179

23
DRAGON☐
FOUNTAIN☐

184
183 186
185 187

182

22
FOUNTAIN OF☐
NEPTUNE☐

180

181

N

RESERVOIRS

☐ ☒ Group
■ Statue
▲ Term
● Metal vase
○ Marble vase

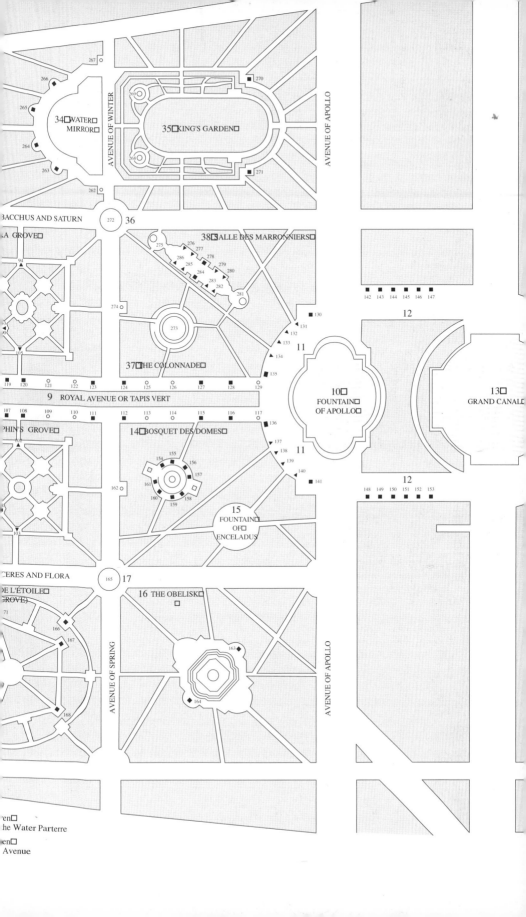

267

266

265

34 WATER MIRROR

264

263

262

AVENUE OF WINTER

269

35 KING'S GARDEN

268

270

271

AVENUE OF APOLLO

BACCHUS AND SATURN

272 36

A GROVE

275

38 SALLE DES MARRONNIERS

276 277
278
286 285 279
284 280
283
282
281

274

273

37 THE COLONNADE

130
131
132
133
11
134

135

142 143 144 145 146 147

12

10 FOUNTAIN OF APOLLO

13 GRAND CANAL

94

105

119 120 121 122 123 124 125 126 127 128 129

9 ROYAL AVENUE OR TAPIS VERT

107 108 109 110 111 112 113 114 115 116 117

136

PHIN'S GROVE

14 BOSQUET DES DOMES

137
138
11
139

140

141

12

148 149 150 151 152 153

102

154 155
156
157
162 161
160 158
159

15
FOUNTAIN
OF
ENCELADUS

CERES AND FLORA

165 17

DE L'ÉTOILE
GROVE)

16 THE OBELISK

71

166

167

163

AVENUE OF SPRING

168

164

AVENUE OF APOLLO

ren
he Water Parterre

en
Avenue